Discover Me

By Phyllis Shulman

Cover photo by Suzy Gorman
Drawings by Paul Baab
Editing by Susan Caba

Printed in the United States of America

Published by WingSpan Press, Livermore, CA
www.wingspanpress.com

The WingSpan name, logo and colophon are the trademarks of WingSpan Publishing.

EAN 1-978-59594-066-7
ISBN 1-59594-066-9

First edition 2006

Library of Congress Control Number 2006905077

Dedication

I'd like to dedicate this book to my Three Jewels. My husband Marty, who allows me to be me. And my two sons, Greg and Josh, who have given me more material than I ever bargained for.

I hate going shopping for clothes when I need new clothes so badly that I have nothing to wear shopping.

Foreword

I can't believe I've had this book on the back burner for twelve years ... enough already! When I went back to stand-up in the early nineties I thought this "I Hate" shtick would be my hook ... think again. I thought I would just include this little book in my big autobiography ... well, the big autobiography isn't written, yet. Now that my kids are teenagers, I decided it was time to finish at least this chapter.

When I read this book it makes me realize how fast our lives rush by us. As a family it's mind-blowing to think of all the different haircuts and hair colors we've been through, the clothes we loved, bought, hated and discarded, the shared meals, the dirty dishes and the laundry. We've gone from junk eaters to eating healthy. My kids have gone from toddlers who clung to and needed me, to "Mom, please don't come over and say hi to me and my friends when you see us at the mall." Life is too short to sit around thinking of all the things to hate. So I've done it for you.

Now don't take this book too seriously. Your hates can change. When I was a kid, I used to hate September because summer was over. Now, I love it ... close the pools, open the schools and get my kids out of my hair! It's the same with snow. When I was a kid, I loved it. Now that I'm older, it just messes up my plans.

So, kick back, turn on the answering machine, turn off the TV (if you can find the remote) and let me share the things I love to hate!

Food: Love It, Hate It

Eating is one of my favorite hobbies -- okay, it is my favorite hobby. I have never given any one subject more thought.

Should I eat?

How much should I eat?

When should I eat?

How guilty am I going to feel when I eat?

Honestly, it's an all-day stream-of-consciousness video in my head:

"A muffin would be good, a muffin and coffee -- with cream, I can't stand coffee without real cream ... you know you don't need cream. And muffins are filled with fat, you might as well eat cake. Cake, I really do like cake, I wonder if there is any Sarah Lee in the freezer? No! You can't have cake, have fruit, have an apple or an orange, my God, I already inhaled the muffin. ... I should have some protein, maybe some soy nuts, Yech! I hate soy nuts, I'll have peanut

butter, a tablespoon of peanut butter --
with a sprinkling of chocolate chips. I'll zap
it in the microwave, so the chips will melt.
... What's for lunch? I really want a burger
and fries, but turkey on whole wheat would
be better ... I ate too much. I really wasn't
hungry. I'm stuffed. I feel miserable and
fat. ... What's to snack on? Don't eat now,
it's too close to bedtime. But there are two
pieces of leftover pizza. The pizza wasn't
even that good, the only good thing, it was
delivered. It won't be any better tomorrow,
and you know you'll eat it then. Okay, but
I'll work out for two hours tomorrow. Oh
my God! Tomorrow! What are we going to
have for dinner tomorrow? I'll have to go
shopping..."

All day long, my brain doesn't stop
with the food issues. If thinking about
food burned calories, I'd be Paris Hilton.
So here's a few things I hate about food --
which is still the love of my life.

I hate being at a party with beautiful,
skinny people and no one else is hanging
out at the buffet table. I hate it that the
beautiful people are picking at the raw
cauliflower while I'm snarfing down the
cheesy fat bombs. I hate that the hostess

puts the cut fruit right next to the plate of gooey brownies. I hate being the only one with hot sauce from the chicken wings dripping down my chin.

I hate it that my husband eats totally healthy when we're out with other people -- and then goes home to a pint of ice cream, followed by a two-sleeve Oreo chaser.

I hate it that the burger joints offer a new toy every few days. Here's my kids' order: "Okay, I'll have a toy, a cheeseburger and French fries." What's really sick is that I have driven through for toys, just to shut them up. "Two Barney's, with cheese, please."

I hate it when the drive-thru line at Burger Boy is wrapped around the building and I make the judgment call that parking and going in will be faster. When I finally get to the counter, I see the blue Volvo that would have been behind me pulling away from the pick-up window. I hate that. Almost as much as I hate when I'm trying to make a left turn into the drive-thru line and there is a stream of traffic making right turns into the line -- and I was really there first!

I hate it when I eat my kids' cold fries and leftover cheeseburgers. What a waste of calories! The hardest thing about parenting is driving home from McBurger and not dipping into those salty, greasy French fries.

I hate it when I miss a meal, which isn't very often. I feel like I've got to make up for it the rest of the day. On the other hand, I hate it when I'm not hungry and I eat anyway, just for entertainment.

I hate that I eat fast. You're supposed to eat slowly, to give your stomach twenty minutes to tell your brain that you're full. Twenty minutes into my meal, my brain is telling my stomach, "Eat, fool, the food is getting cold!"

I hate when you're trying to pick a restaurant with someone and they say, "Oh, you choose, I don't care."
Me: "Okay, how about Italian?"
Them: "No, no. I had Italian last night."
Me: "Okay, let's go Chinese."
Them: "I don't eat Chinese any more -- too much MSG."
Me: "What are you in the mood for?"
Them: "Anything, really. You choose."

I hate going to a restaurant with someone and whatever they order, it looks better than what I ordered. I hate it when I see my hot food is ready to be delivered to my table and Stan, my "server" is nowhere in sight. Meanwhile, my food is congealing under the warming hood.

Worse yet, when my food is delivered hot, it never fails that a friend happens along and stops to chat -- just long enough for the food to cool off. I'm like, Hel-lo, Good-bye!

I hate it when I'm just diving into a plate of spaghetti and the waiter comes by to ask how it is. I look up with the noodles hanging out and grunt, and we nod at each other as if to acknowledge that I can't stuff it in my mouth fast enough. I hate that.

What I really hate is when I spend good money on something that sounds delicious but really stinks. I keep chomping away, hoping it will taste better on the next bite.

I hate it when I ask for a doggy bag and then leave it in the restaurant. I was planning on eating the leftovers during the drive home. Now, if I do remember to take it – and don't eat it on the way home – I hate when I leave it in the car overnight. Yuck! I really don't want my car to smell like linguine and clams. I'll always go for the new leather smell over the odor of spoiled leftovers.

I hate people who stock up on Sweet 'n Lows at restaurants. When I was a kid, my mother chose restaurants based on how they distributed the sugar substitutes. "Oh no, we can't eat there," she'd say. "The waitress only hands you two at a time from her apron." Same thing with the little sealed packets of jelly. We had to eat at places that put the sugar and jelly on the table. I was eighteen before I realized you could actually buy Sweet 'n Low at the grocery store and that jelly came in a jar.

I hate it when my bananas get over-ripe and those little fruit flies are all over the kitchen.

I love eating poppy-seed bagels but I hate it that I have to check my teeth afterwards. Otherwise I go around looking like something from Deliverance.

I hate that we're supposed to eat six to eight servings a day of fruits and vegetables. I don't think I've ever eaten an apple and said, "Jeez, that was good -- I've got to have another one." I've never in my life yelled to my husband, "Honey, I'm getting ready to raid the refrigerator -- hide that broccoli!" On the other hand, I've often consumed a big bag of Doritos, licked my lips and thought, "I could do another half-bag, easy."

I hate watching cooking shows, especially the ones that emphasize healthy gourmet food. My stomach is growling, my mouth is watering and I haven't even heard of half the ingredients. I get so hungry watching, I end up consuming three boxes of reduced fat cookies.

Speaking of reduced fat, I hate it when all I'm eating is low fat, fat-free, no fat -- and all I'm doing is gaining weight!

I hate it when I pull out my Nutri-System pcn to take notes at my Weight Watchers meeting. Flip a coin – is it going to be LA Weight Loss this week or South Beach diet. Pick a coast, cross your fingers and maybe you'll lose a few pounds.

I hate it when the kids are yelling, "I want Taco Smell." "I want Crap in the Box." I'm like, "Can't you boys make up your minds?" Oy, this menu planning! One night, I'm embarrassed to tell you, I had three different delivery guys at home. One kid wanted one kind of pizza, one kid wanted another kind of pizza, and I wanted Chinese. And if you don't think that's difficult, try coordinating those delivery times so that you can eat as a family!

And then Marty comes home. He's like, "When you had the kitchen redone, you had to have the best of everything. You don't even cook!" I'm like, "That's right, honey. Would you like the thin crust or the thick crust? Would you like a little chicken chow mein, egg foo yon or the moo goo guy pan?"

I hate it when I blow a great day of dieting ten minutes before bedtime.

I hate it when my kids want some of my gourmet diet TV dinner. "Can I please have these three ounces of food to myself?" If I cooked them the same meal from scratch, they wouldn't touch it.

I hate it when I play raquetball for two hours, then reward myself with a corned beef sandwich and potato salad.

I can't stand that my before diet picture makes me look thinner than my after picture.

I hate that we're supposed to drink six to eight glasses of water a day. Now I don't have time to eat -- I spend half my time looking for a john. Last week I was up six gallons.

I hate it that I keep a running mental inventory of what's in my refrigerator and pantry. I toss and turn in bed, knowing there is a bag of Chips Ahoy in the back left corner of the cupboard. I'm not happy until I get up and polish them off, with a half-quart of low-fat milk.

What I really hate? I hate it when the cupboards are full, but there's nothing to eat.

Daily Aggravations

Every day, a bazillion things get on my nerves. You know – these are the miscellaneous annoyances that punctuate your life. Some are fleeting but others just stay with me for hours, and I hate that.

I hate when I'm trying to throw a trashcan away – and the collectors won't pick it up for weeks and weeks. I have to flag them down with a couple cold six-packs to make them happy.

I hate reading magazines at the doctor's office, turning the page only to see that the final page is missing. I especially hate this when the final page contained a recipe that I was going to tear out for myself. I hate short lines at the grocery store because it doesn't give me enough time to read my trashy magazines and I have to end up buying the darn things. Which is why I love the gyno's office, because it's always a two-hour wait and I can catch up on all my magazine reading. God forbid the nurse calls me in the middle of a juicy article; I can always finish it while waiting an additional 20 minutes with my feet up in the cold stirrups.

Speaking of being stuck, I hate being stuck behind someone at airport security who is so over-pierced they hold up the whole line taking various bits of metal out of their body. This is particularly galling when I'm standing there barefoot, my pants around my ankles because I've taken off my belt and suffering an anxiety attack wondering if my underwire bra is going to result in a strip search.

I hate conversations that begin, "Hey, you know what you need to do?" Invariably, those conversations end with "But I don't have to tell you what you should do."

I hate when my dental hygienist tries to carry on a conversation like I don't have her two hands in my mouth. "Mmmpff, grgrrgmggle, pflejmml." This is actual torture – two women not being able to have conversation for 45 minutes. It's almost as bad as my gynecologist making small talk while I've got feet in the stirrups with my toes up his nose.

I can't figure out whether I'm under-watering my plants or over-watering them. I hate that.

Personalized license plates. Cute. Sometimes. But I hate it when the owner of an expensive car brags about it on the license plates – "MY BENZ" or "MY 450SL." The most obnoxious I ever saw was R2JAGS. Just in case passers-by weren't impressed enough that you have one Jaguar, you let them know you have two! It made me want 2 B Sick.

I hate giving a beautiful, expensive wedding gift and finding out three months later – usually before the thank-you note has arrived – that the couple is divorcing. In fact, I hate giving gifts for second and third marriages. I'm thinking of asking for pre-nuptial agreements – the marriage lasts less than five years, I get my gift back.

I really hate lies. So I have to confess. When I said I've never eaten an apple and craved another, I lied. I just ate two candy apples that were out of sight! Now I've got to floss nuts and caramel out of my teeth. I hate that, too.

I hate being last in a very long line, but especially at places like Disneyland where they try to fool you into thinking the line is shorter by making it zigzag around corners.

I get very annoyed with people who pull out an entire family photo album when all I've asked is to see a picture of their kids. I meant one picture!

I hate being sworn to secrecy when someone is giving me a hot scoop. What's the point of gossip if you can't tell anyone? On the other hand, I hate even more being the last to know.

Thank You Soooo Much For...

- [ ] The Beautiful Expensive Birthday Present
- [ ] The Not So Beautiful Inexpensive Birthday Present.

I Can't Wait To...

- [ ] Use it
- [ ] Wear it
- [ ] Read It
- [ ] Eat it
- [ ] Put Batteries in it
- [ ] Return it
- [ ] Give it to my cleaning lady

Hey Listen, it wasn't about the presents, you may not have gotten me anything which is fine, it was just about everyone getting together and having a good time.

It was great to see you, you looked ...

- [ ] Fabulous
- [ ] Not So Fabulous
- [ ] A Little Heavy
- [ ] Too Thin
- [ ] A Bit Over Dressed
- [ ] Slightly Underdressed

Love, Phyllis

P.S. I'd really appreciate if you'd help me fill out these thank you notes because it's been a busy weekend. Hope you had a good time, because I know I did!

Thank-you notes -- I hate writing them. You know they go right in the trash as soon as they read. This is a multiple-choice thank you after one of my birthday parties.

15

I hate mail that says "Open Immediately." You know it's either bad news or junk.

I hate people who shorten my name the minute they meet me. My husband and I will be introduced at a party as Phyllis and Marty. The person turns around and is, like, "Oh Phil, Mar, what a pleasure." Haven't known the person ten seconds and already I don't like him.

I can't help noticing – and I hate it – when people don't recycle. Especially if I go to a bar or restaurant and they are pitching tons of bottles and plastic. I've just ruined a new manicure scrubbing out a peanut jar I'm going to discard. If I'm going to obsess and feel guilty about my trash, I want everyone else to feel guilty about theirs!

I hate bald guys with ponytails. "You're bald, guy! Face it, life isn't fair. But you don't look hipper with that tail hanging from a bald pate." To me it looks like half of a Davy Crockett hat.

I'm resentful when I have to get down on my hands and knees at a cocktail party to look for someone's contact lens. I feel like saying, "Look, my husband's an optometrist. Come on down to the office and we'll give you a deal. Can I stand up now?"

I hate waiting for change of a nickel or less.

I hate stopping at gas stations when my kids are in the car. These places are like mini-malls – you can get everything from baseball caps to movies to instant cameras. Of course, if you want full-service gas or need your oil checked, forget about it!

I hate it that everyone is in search of the perfect parking space.

It's funny, because in this country we spend billions of dollars on diet and exercise but when we go to the mall, we have to get the closest parking spot.

"Let me just keep circling the lot because I have to walk in and get my new Nordic Track and a new exercise video. Maybe I'll get Cindy Crawford this time and really get depressed."

Cindy has actually been good for me because I turn her on and she is so gorgeous that I am too depressed to eat. I just pop a Xanax and a Prozac and call it a day.

If you really want to have some fun when you do get that perfect parking spot – you know, the one right next to the handicapped and it's not handicapped, the one where the whole carload of kids goes crazy yelling, "Oh yeah, Mom. Here. Stop. Pull in. Got it. Cool." What I do is get out and just kind of hang around the trunk of my car holding my keys. Then I watch everybody slam on their brakes and mouth "Are you leaving?" to me. No, sorry, I'm not. Keep circling. Oh well, it's cheap entertainment.

By the way, I hate driving a mini-van. I only got it for my kids, so I feel perfectly justified reminding them how they'll have to care for me when I'm old and drooling. "You'll have to wipe my face and change my diapers. Don't you even think about putting me in a nursing home! I do everything for you!" Guilt – don't you love it?

I find it irritating when celebrities brag about working out for four hours a day. I'd love to have that much time to work out (or do anything, for that matter). Do they ever have to say, "Let's see, I've got forty free minutes – should I exercise, mop the kitchen, run to the grocery, or write my bills?

I hate invisible fences. The other morning, two pit bulls charged me from their owner's front porch. I hate having to pray that something I couldn't see was going to save me.

I hate when I'm at a party and the family dog puts his nose right between my legs. Well, maybe I don't hate it that much ... good boy, Rocky, good boy!

Holidays, now here's a fruitful category for annoyance.

As a kid, I loved holidays. Now that I'm the grown-up, they're too much work. Get the food, buy new clothes, scrub the house and hunt for the decorations. Give up the hunt and buy new decorations. Scrub the kids, spot-clean the house where it's gotten dirty in the past twelve hours, cook the food, arrange and display it. Threaten the kids and the dog with death if any of them slobber over the appetizers. Shower, dress, check the appetizers for slobber. Greet the guests, entertain, open the gifts and coo over them, while wondering where they can be returned. Say goodbye, clean up the mess, take down the decorations, eat all the leftovers and gain five pounds, and collapse.

I say I loved holidays as a kid. But now that I think about it, my memories of the Jewish holidays aren't all that pleasant. I always had to wear new wool clothes, even when the holidays fell in September and the weather was hot and sticky. My clothes itched all through services and all the old people smelled like mothballs and had bad breath from fasting and not brushing their teeth. Afterwards, we got back into a steaming car, drove to my grandmother's sweltering apartment and ate hot soup. Happy New Year!

Speaking of holidays, I hate it that every year we have a family argument over who will host the breaking of the Yom Kippur fast. What I hate about it is that, in reality, nobody fasts.

I hate it when people hang a different holiday banner next to their front door every month. Even worse, I can't stand those holiday wrappers for mailboxes. What's the point? The mailman certainly doesn't need to be reminded which holiday is up next – he's got catalogs to do that.

I hate it that the Super Bowl now qualifies as a national holiday. Every year, the pressure is on to have a Super Bowl party – and I hate football!

I can't stand people who leave their Christmas lights on through May.

I hate people with a lot of nerve. When my father died, some lady came to pay her respects. She stayed for lunch and dinner. She came back for lunch the next day and was anticipating staying for dinner. My brother-in-law politely informed her that she had paid enough respect and thanked her for coming. I told him, "Maybe she was between jobs," I said, "and needed a couple of free meals."

"Nope," said my brother-in-law, "I think she was in between funerals."

I hate owning. Renting is so much easier. Rent-a-Kid is definitely the way to go. Nieces-for-a-Weekend was heaven! Full-time boys of my own – not heaven. Even my husband was more fun when I was renting him. Now that I own him, the thrill is gone.

Renting a car. That's fun. Drive it as hard as you can. Let the kids eat French fries to their hearts' content. Same thing with a hotel. "That's okay, honey, if you leave the pizza on the nightstand. Go ahead, jump on the bed. No, no, no, Mommy doesn't care if your wet bathing suit is soaking the carpet. Oh yeah, that lamp shade does make a great helmet, honey."

One thing I do hate renting is bowling shoes. Yuck! Double Yuck! Does the whole bowling alley have to know I wear a size 11 shoe?

I hate it when my relatives start bragging about how well they're doing financially and they owe me money.

I hate it when I've returned someone's wave and then realized he wasn't waving at me. I hate it even more when I'm only halfway through the wave when the realization hits me – do I finish the wave or pretend I'm fixing my hair?

Adventures With
The Late, Great

I hate it when people tell you their long, boring celebrity stories...

I believe it was January 1991 when my sister Susan and I .had the good fortune to meet the late, great Mr. Rodney Dangerfield.

Every year we would meet a group of friends and relatives in Las Vegas for Super Bowl weekend. Not that we're big football fans—it's just that one year we were planning a trip to Vegas and our travel agents asked if we wanted to go Super Bowl weekend and we said, "Why not?" We thought it would be more exciting than just any weekend in January. Besides, I was a blackjack addict and I knew the tables would be empty during the game.

Between my sister and me, we were sure to have enough laughs. My sister is funnier than me—she's so dry, we call her The Desert. We were there with cousins from California and two gay friends from San Francisco. No Vegas trip was complete until I peed in my pants which, to me, is like the orgasm of laughing.

So this late Saturday afternoon, Susan and I are shopping in the Arcade at the old MGM Hotel, where we were staying. A salesgirl says, very nonchalantly, "Oh, there goes Rodney Dangerfield." Susan and I just threw down the handbags we were looking at and ran to tackle Rodney.

He was wearing a white bathrobe and told us he was on the way to workout and get a massage. I was so excited, I blurted out that I would give him a massage. We were beside ourselves. I couldn't stop quoting him. (To my credit, I never said, "I don't get any respect." Because how many times had he heard that?) I told him I'd seen him every time he was in St. Louis because my husband loved him and didn't care for most comics. I told it would be "unbelievable" if we could get a picture of us all together to give my husband, who doesn't fly and wasn't in Vegas. He gives us his room number and tells us to meet him up in his suite in about an hour.

My sister and I are pinching ourselves, we're higher than two kites, to mix a metaphor. I called Marty—he can't believe our luck. Then we phone the other four people in Vegas with us, gushing that we can all go up to Rodney Dangerfield's room for autographs and pictures. Do you believe it—every single one of them said, "Oh, just go ahead and call us when you're done, then we can all meet up for dinner."

I couldn't believe it. This is one of my idols and everyone is acting like we met someone from show business like John Davidson, Alex Trebeck or Chuck Woolery—someone I couldn't care less if I ever met or not.

Naturally, we arrived at Rodney's suite early. He wasn't back from his massage, so we just killed time in front of his suite. Turned out the suite across the hall was open, so we took a quick tour, self-guided, if you know what I mean. It was everything a Vegas suite should be. It was knocked-out gorgeous like something from Architectural Digest, just beautiful, all in beiges and whites. I believe I put a really pretty ashtray in my purse (those were the old days, when I would steal something and could justify it. Not anymore. I wouldn't take a single Sweet 'N Low and you can put me under oath on that.) A few minutes later, Rodney and his bag boy came along, and the four of us walk into his suite together.

What a shock! His suite is a piece of garbage compared to the one across the hall. It's leftover from the Seventies, all royal blue and dark bamboo furniture. I always try to be complimentary, so I say, "Hey, this is really nice!" Rodney's bag boy nudges him and winks, like "what a loser." So I said, "Okay, make fun of the Hoosiers from St. Louis. But if you want to know the truth, this place is crap. You should see the pad across the hall." Rodney, in typical Rodney style, says "Well, what do I need? I mean, what do I really need? This is good enough for me!"

We had a nice conversation about stand-up, took some pictures and left, my sister and me still on our high. We had his phone number, so we called him all weekend bugging him to impress people we would meet. I don't remember when we met him, but I can tell you when he died—Oct. 5, 2004, my niece Emily's birthday and the day I finally quit smoking for good. I was grateful for our encounter with the man who gets nothing but my respect.

I'd just like to thank the Comedy Gods for giving me the opportunity to have this little encounter with a comedy great. In case anyone is listening or cares, Phyllis Diller is on my list of people I'd like to share a conversation with. Oh! I just remembered I did pass George Burns on the street in New York. He had a young blond on his arm and my girlfriend grabbed me and said, "Gracie would turn over in her grave." Say goodnight, Gracie.

Entertainment

I don't know anyone who doesn't enjoy a good concert, movie or play. I just pray that once I'm seated, the person next to me doesn't arrive with a box of Kleenex and a fifth of cough syrup. Even worse, the person behind me won't shut his trap during the whole performance. I feel like saying, "Listen, pal, I didn't spend six bucks to park, four dollars for this drink and $75 for this ticket to listen to you."

I love being entertained. But here's a list of "hates" that can sometimes foul up my entertainment plans.

I hate when I go to a movie and I've already seen all the funny parts fifteen times in the previews.

I hate it when I tell the cashier at the movies that I need one senior citizen ticket and she believes me.

I hate it when they list the top ten albums in the newspaper. Can we switch it to CDs already? And, please, don't invent anything to replace the compact disc player. I've already bought enough albums, eight-tracks, cassettes and CDs. I've spent enough already!

Great, glad they listened. Now my kids have to have IPods. Like I said, I've spent enough already! I hate that.

I hate it when I take my kids to the video store and the DVD they want is not for rent, only for sale!

I hate it when a guy tries to pick me up at a bar and he's too cheap to buy me a drink. I hate it when a guy does buy me a drink and I can't get rid of him. One lousy $4 drink and he thinks he owns me for the rest of the week.

I hate it when a guy tells me he's separated. Right! "You're here and your wife is at home."

I hate women who swear their husbands would never cheat on them. These are the same men who have a permanent nookie suite at the Ritz Carlton.

I hate guys that hit on women when they're pregnant. Where were you when we

31

were single? Guys love pregnant women. They must feel safe from all commitments or future blood tests. What bums!

I hate it when you're dating someone you like and after a few months, he remembers to tell you that he's married. "Well, that's okay. I forgot to tell you about my genital herpes."

I hate camping. Holiday Inn is roughing it for me. The last time we were on vacation, my seven-year-old said, "Mom, I know why you are so happy when we are on vacation – because a maid comes every day."

I hate leaving a great party to go to one that sucks.

I hate it that my husband has all his deadbeat friends over to watch every sporting event on television. One's eating potato salad out of the carton, one's got beer cans lying all over the floor and one's tying up my phone line with his bookie. At least one came first class – he changed his underwear.

I hate going to a baseball or football game when the food and souvenirs cost more than the ticket.

I hate knowing that no one ever uses the restrooms at public swimming pools. Why don't they just put the toilet paper next to the pool steps?

I hate asking for directions and the guy says, "Don't worry, you can't miss it." Of course, I miss it. I hate that.

Vegas. I love Vegas. But I hate it when you ask someone how she did gambling and she gives you her life story. "Well, I was up $1,800 on the craps table and I should never have started playing Blackjack. If it hadn't started raining, I would have left the casino. You wouldn't believe how bad I started going. I had two aces and I split them and got two twos." I wish I had a dollar for every time I've heard that story or one just as boring.

Then I hate it when someone says he lost $500 – but he had a great time! Oh, really? What else is a good time to you – funerals? Car accidents?

I hate craps. If I play the Do, they Don't. If I play the Don't, they Do. I recently got a fortune cookie that said, "He who gambles picks his own pocket." I wish that cookie had popped up twenty years ago.

I hate that riverboat gambling has come to my hometown, St. Louis. Now on Saturday nights, it's "Honey, do you want to go to the boat or do you want to go to a movie and save a couple hundred dollars?"

I hate it when they publish the pictures of slot machine winners in the newspaper. You never hear about the losers – "I lost my trailer, my dog, my wife and my dentures. I'm in Gamblers Anonymous for the rest of my life." Now, there's a story!

I hate it when I lose $1,200 in Vegas, but I'm too cheap to get a bellboy to carry my bags. I end up throwing my back out. What a town!

I hate it when I'm playing Blackjack and I get 20 and the dealer draws 21. I hate it when I have Blackjack and the dealer has an ace showing. I hate it when I split two eights. Well, that's another whole book: "Things I Hate While Playing Blackjack."

Family Life and the Domestic Scene

I hate to complain, but a woman with a home can't even sit on the toilet and have a moment's rest. You look around and think, "God, those shower doors need to be scrubbed, the toilet paper needs to be changed, the baseboards are filthy, the carpet needs to be shampooed, the wallpaper is filthy, the bathtub is scum." If it's not the inside of the house, something has to be cut or raked outside. Don't get me wrong. I love my family and home. But there's always someone or something that needs to be cleaned, washed, bought, watched, fed, scrubbed, repaired, cooked, warmed up, nursed or loved. It's all worth it. But here are some of the things I hate about the whole scene. (Come on in, but please don't trip over the roller blades.)

I hate when other people have perfectly clean jelly jars, with no traces of peanut butter or margarine mixed in with the jelly.

I hate it when I have to make appointments with my kids and husband to vacuum around their television schedules. Thank God they have the common courtesy to lift their feet for the vacuum.

I hate it when someone's garage is cleaner than my house.

I hate leaving my husband to baby-sit the kids when the house is clean. He sits on the sofa and watches them destroy the house. When I come home, there's peanut butter on the dog and jelly on the walls. I'm so glad I got a chance to get away from it all. When I leave now, I just yell, "Don't clean up anything. I want to be able to recognize the place when I get home."

I hate it when the sun comes out while I am cleaning my house. I never get done. It goes much faster when I do it at night or with my sunglasses on.

My cleaning lady can't see and she never turns on a light or opens the blinds. Do I really think I'm getting my money's worth? I hate that.

I hate it that they don't make those big toilet paper rolls like you see in restaurants and bars for residential use. I'm the one always changing the toilet paper in the house.

I hate it when I spend an hour and a half watering my lawn and, as soon as I'm finished, it rains.

I hate when I'm cleaning up a big tree mess in my driveway—and it's from my neighbor's tree.

I hate looking at display homes. Everything is brand new and clean. It makes me want to come home and put a match to my house. My décor is "early toddler."

I hate it that I can't walk into my walk-in closet.

I hate stain resistant carpeting—because it isn't. Whoever invented it has never met my husband, kids and dogs.

I hate having my carpets cleaned. The very next day, the dog throws up all over the place—it never fails!

I hate it that I have three televisions and two DVDs and, between my kids and my husband, I never get to watch anything I want.

I hate laundry. It never ends. Even if you think you are finally caught up, look at your family and you're looking at another load of laundry.

I hate having only one outfit to choose from because everything else is dirty.

I hate it when my special-order furniture is delivered and I hate it. It's bad enough when you don't like the new furniture that's delivered off the showroom floor. No, me, I have to hate something I waited eight to twelve weeks to have delivered. And then, to top it off, I hear my husband's mouth: "What do you think you are, a decorator?" "No, honey, you're right," I say. "Did I tell you I also hate the wallpaper I picked for the kitchen?"

I hate it when I've emptied the entire dishwasher and discover the dishes haven't been washed. I've just put away a whole load of dirty dishes! Yuk!

And then there's grocery shopping. Now there's a fertile field for hates.

I hate it when I try to bring all my groceries into the house in one trip. It would have been faster to make two trips in the first place. Then I wouldn't have to clean up the apple juice that spilled all over the kitchen floor.

I hate it when I put something in the freezer that was intended for the refrigerator. Or worse, when I stick the ice cream in the pantry.

Coupons—I hate 'em. They never work for me. I've either left them at home, bought the wrong size, or let them expire.

I hate it when I'm polite at the deli counter and let someone go in front of me. They end up ordering for a Super Bowl party for 45, when all I wanted was a half-pound of turkey.

I hate the way some people act in the grocery store. The other day, a man was picking and eating the grapes. I'm like, "Excuse me, Pop, I don't want to disrupt your lunch, but I'm a cash customer here."

I hate it when my ice cream melts in the express line.

I hate it when I'm standing in line at the grocery store with a full cart and someone comes up behind me with just bread and milk. Naturally, I feel obligated to let the bread and milk lady go ahead of me. How was I to know she'd be paying with the money she took from her kid's piggy bank— "this makes 98 cents, this makes 99 cents, this make a dollar..."

I hate the sale flyers that come in the Sunday paper. When it's on sale, I don't need it. When I need it, it's not on sale.

I hate rebates, especially for only $1. After I put a 39-cent stamp on it, I end up being ahead a whopping 61 cents. "Call my stockbroker. How's NASDAQ doing today?"

I hate return lines at discount stores. They're so long. By the time I make the exchange, my kids have grown into a different size.

I hate when I run into the grocery store for just bread and milk and end up spending $75. I had no idea when I had kids that they were going to be hungry and thirsty for the rest of their lives.

Kids, Ya Gotta Love 'Em

What can I say—I love my kids. And I can't help sharing, as you can see by this email exchange with my niece, who calls me Cousin Maven.

Cousin Maven:
    I just wanted to send you some pictures of my beautiful little girl - Alexandra (but we call her Lexi). She is without a doubt the greatest thing I've ever done. If I'd known how much I love being a Mom, I would have done this years ago.
    I'm happy to hear that you're still pursuing your comedy career - I'm still convinced that you will make it big one day. Did you try out for Last Comic Standing? I would have loved to have seen YOU in that house...oy vey!
Lots of love.
Lauren

Lauren,

I'm just beaming for you...So glad for all your happiness. She's gorgeous. Mazel Tov! Mazel Tov! Mazel Tov! I couldn't be happier for you and your family. I see a lot of you in Lexi. Please put me down for her first manicure and pedicure—my treat.

Let Lexi know that you will definitely need her in your senior years for diaper changes, facial hair removal and denture cleanings.

Enjoy, because when they get to be teenagers, they're not around. I say, "Give your kid a credit card, a cell phone, and a car and you never have to see them." Which I'm kinda enjoying now because the party was always at my house.

Greg has been driving since last July. He just goes from one hobby to another until he collects every accessory he needs and then moves on to the next adventure. The past couple of years it's been racquetball, golf (he's on the team at school), rock-climbing, skiing—and I've got the Mastercharge bills to prove it. I actually have a rock wall in my garage that he begged for and I haven't seen him on it once. We went from a two-car garage to a one and now we're a three-car family.

Josh is the funny one...Josh-man is actually our cook. He turned into a chef and that makes all of us happy campers. He'll probably go to culinary school. He is into paint-balling, playing Hold-em poker, and having harmless fun with his friends.

My kids are happy, they hang with their friends and do what 16- and 17-year-old Jewish boys do who aren't getting into trouble....... Tank God! The worst that's happened so far is Greg has gotten a couple speeding tickets that Marty doesn't know about because I had them fixed. They did get busted this summer for toilet-papering some houses in the neighborhood. They asked me if I ever did it. I said "Yes, once, and why do you think we don't have any trees in our front yard?"

So now, down to the comedy career question:

You know, my whole life, all I ever really wanted to be the best at was standup comedy. You mentioned "Last Comic Standing." Everywhere I go, people ask me why I'm not on that show. I didn't hear about any try-outs this year and comedy contests are tough—it's not about being funny sometimes. Sometimes, it's what the producers are looking for. ... Anyway, back to the story. In 1986, I decided I was going to be famous and I started doing open mike nights at a comedy club here in St. Louis. I had Marty all excited that I was going to be the next Joan Rivers and have my own sit-com ... blah, blah, blah.

I assured him I never wanted kids because I went through every uglystage you could imagine in my own childhood and I didn't want to put my own flesh and blood through that.

I had a horrible act at the time. I hated every minute of it. I sucked, my act sucked, but I was sure this was the way to Fame and Fortune.

One summer night, I'm on stage and Marty is in the audience. I got cotton-mouthsoooooooobad I could not speak. It was like I smoked 18 joints. The strangest thing happened. Right there and then, I decided I wanted a baby.

So I got off stage and I went over to Marty and I said, "You're not going to believe this but I want to get pregnant."He looked disappointed, like "You mean we're not going to Hollywood and I'm not quitting work?"

I said "Marty, it's the weirdest thing—all of sudden I want a baby!"He looked at me and said, "Whatever you want."

Which is a moment in our marriage that I have to remember on bad days, because I could have taken bites from his face, he looked so sweet. Anyway, the next summer Greg was born and that kid has never had an ugly day in his life, lucky guy.

Like the Jewish mothers we are, our kids will come first and we will have no regrets. Isn't that the name of a song?

Gotta go, the kids want on the computer.

Love,
Cousin Maven

One day, when my boys were still in diapers, something scary occurred to me. These guys are going to grow up and get married.I'm going to have two daughters-in-law who will hate me. I'm working towards being a mother-in-law. How depressing. Oh, well. I hear boys are less expensive to raise. I guess when they get older, they can split pairs of earrings. I can't wait. I'll be so proud to see my boys in earrings. On the other hand, who else would say, "Gee, Mom, you got a wiggly tussie," or tell you, "You know, Mom, spiders can have kids and they don't even have to be married."

Well, there are a few things about my kids that bug me.

I hate it when my son yells from the bathroom, "Mommy, I'm taking a bath in the shower." I yell back, "Honey, take that washrag out of the drain. The carpet is still mildewed from your last bath in the shower."

I hate it when one of my kids is good and the other one is bad. God forbid they could be good at the same time!

I hate buying dress clothes for my kids. At least with expensive sneakers, they wear them for three months.

I hate it when my kid presses the emergency stop button on the elevator. This is not my idea of fun, being trapped in an elevator for an hour with two kids and three skinheads.

I hate going out to dinner without my kids – and I get seated around a bunch of other people's kids.

I hate the word "Mom," as in:
"Mom, I have a dribble in my pants."
"Mom, get me a drink."
"Mom, wipe my tussie."
"Mom, I pooped in my pants."
"Mom, Joshie hit me."
"Mom, I'm hungry."
"Mom, watch me swing."
"Mom, Greg kicked me."
"Mom, Josh is drinking your nail polish remover."

I hate it that kids don't come with warning labels:

Caution! Beware! Warning!
Will require spurts of extremely high energy.
Will fight with siblings.
Will think farting and burping is funny.
Will plead and beg until you give in just because you can't take it anymore.
Will tend to have same expensive tastes as parents.

I hate waiting for my kids to fall asleep so I can score with their dad. By the time they're asleep, we're too tired.

I hate it when my kids fart in the carwash. On purpose. What comedians!

I hate it when a new friend comes over for coffee and my kids throw their hamster on the kitchen table, right where we're chatting.Cute, huh?
Hamsters—that's another thing I hate. Please tell me one thing these rodents are good for. Ours are just something else in the house that eats and poops that I have to clean up after. And just as soon as I get

the kids to sleep, the hamsters are up. How did I let my kids beg me into this mess?

I hate parents who say, "Well, I only allow my kids to watch television for half-an-hour a day. I filter everything they view." I'm thinking, "You got to be kidding." When my kids are running and jumping off the walls, I'd let them watch the Spice channel if they'd just sit down, shut up and stop fighting for an hour.

I hate it when my kids wake me up at 5 a.m. on Saturday to tell me about the new fort they just built in the living room. "Yeah, Mommy, we took the slats from our bunk beds and glued them together with peanut butter and mayonnaise." Great, guys. Could you just get me a cup of coffee before I go ballistic?

I hate it that, after years of having my parents yell at me to turn down the stereo, now my kids are yelling at me to turn it down.

I hate it when people leave a phone message with my kids and expect me to get it.

I hate cleaning up a mess in one room while my kids are making a bigger mess in another room.

I hate it when I just collapsed on the couch from exhaustion and my kid yells, "Mom, I threw up on the carpet."

Mini-Legos—who invented them? I hate mini-Legos, especially when I'm barefoot. My vacuum clean repairman, however, loves them. As a matter of fact, every time one of my kids has a birthday, he gives them another set.

I hate people who, every time you ask them how their kids are, they reply, "Great. Wonderful. Fantastic." How could these kids be great all the time? It's impossible. Having a kid is like having a puppy for 25 years.

I hate it that I sound like my parents when I correct my kids. "Close the door. What are you doing—cooling off the neighborhood? The air conditioning is on." Or, "Why do you need all these lights on? What do you think—we've got stock in Union Electric?" I swore I'd never say those things.

I hate being such a good mom that I keep buying my kids paint-and-glitter kits so that I have more messes to clean up.

I hate it when people brag about their kids. I never brag about my kids—but they are absolute geniuses. At the age of two, they could read, spell and abbreviate. Sure. They knew the words, "play," "stop" and "eject." And they knew the abbreviations for "fast forward," "rewind" and "record." Brilliant kids, but you'd never hear it from me. "That's right, honey. That's the 'record' button, so if you see anything on TV that will interest you for six hours, let Mommy know and I'll get you a blank tape."

©P.BABB-

I hate it when my kids take a bubble bath and they think the tub is a swimming pool. I'll bet I'm the only mother with a "No Diving" sign in the bathroom. "Honey, be good or it's 'adult swim only.'"

I hate it when my kids laugh at me when I'm trying to be serious. My mother told me, "Someday, your kids will laugh at you just like you're laughing at me." She was right—and I hate that, too.

I hate it when I arrive home at 1 a.m. and my babysitter is sitting on her boyfriend's lap and my kids are still running around.

I hate walking into toy stores with my kids. I get an instant headache. It always reminds me of a scene from a Steve Martin movie. I set up all the rules before we go in. "Listen, guys, we're just running in to buy Daniel's birthday present. So don't beg me for anything because I'm not spending a dime on you." Next scene, you catch us walking to the car with three huge bags of toys and my kids are grinning ear to ear.

I hate it that my kids go to bed at 10:30 p.m. and wake up at 6 a.m. One of my friends told me that real smart kids don't require a lot of sleep and I said, "Really? Then give me a couple of dummies."

I hate it when my kids fall asleep while I'm reading them their bedtime story. I feel like a fool finishing up the book by myself. But I just have to know if Brother and Sister Bear make the Bear Country Little League.

I hate that my boys are so creative—like when they paint the bathroom with my nail polish.

I hate it when I go out for a relaxing lunch alone and am seated right in the midst of four tables with screaming kids.

I hate juice boxes—one big squeeze and I'm mopping the kitchen floor again.

I hate taking my kids to the library. We always check out the maximum amount. Try to find 18 kids' books two weeks later!

Library books, I hate 'em. Especially when I sell one at a garage sale for 25 cents and have to replace it later for $20.

I hate that my kids are little couch potatoes. My biggest fear is walking into my family room in twenty years and finding them still on the couch, watching "Home Alone With Hookers."

I hate the sound of my own voice. As in: "Brush your teeth, please." "Don't play catch with the dog in the house." "Get your dirty hands off the walls." "My bed is not a trampoline." "Don't fight with your brother."

"Eat over your plate." "Lift up the toilet seat." "Don't forget to put the toilet seat down after." "Puh-leeze don't talk with your mouth full." "BRUSH YOUR FACE, WASH YOUR TEETH!" "Don't laugh at me –do what I'm thinking, not what I'm saying!"

Pets may be the only things more aggravating than kids, so I'm throwing in a couple of pet peeves here, for your entertainment.

I hate it that my dog will eat anything but dog food.

I hate it that my dog's haircuts cost more than mine and that she looks cuter than I do.

I hate it when my puppy turns my new Italian loafers into open-toed sandals.

I hate it when my pedigree pooch finally finds her precious spot to poop. It's usually in the neighbor's yard, while she's outside raking leaves.

I hate it when I'm playing ball with my dog and I throw it real far—and she won't go get it. "Fetch, Phyllis, fetch."

I hate it that my veterinarian is more expensive than my pediatrician. My dogs have cost me a fortune. When I got my puppies, my vet drove a Toyota. A few years later, he stepped up to a 300ZX. Now he's driving a Porsche. If these dogs live much longer, he'll be behind the wheel of a Masseratti.

I hate when my dogs bark for five minutes because they heard a doorbell ring on television.

The Telephone

The more advances we make on the telephone, the more I hate it. If a human actually answer the phone these days, I'm shocked. My first reaction is, "Oh, you're there?" And what's the first thing they say? "Yeah, can you hold on a minute?"

And cell phones. Oy, I hate 'em. You're in the grocery store and someone's yelling into their phone, "Yeah, did you want the Bibb or the iceberg? Did you want the bleu cheese or the provel?" Me, yelling at the guy, "NO! I want YOU to go to a PAY PHONE is what I want!"

I hate Caller ID. You can't even give someone an old-fashioned hanger-upper anymore.

I hate it when I have someone's home phone number, work phone number, beeper number, cell phone number—and I still can't get a hold of them.

I hate it when my kids hide the cordless phone in the toilet.

I hate it when my mother puts me on hold. "Call Waiting" should not be available to senior citizens.For them, it's more like "Call Forgetting." When she asks, "Can you hold?" she means forever.

I hate it when I'm gone for six hours and I've forgotten to turn on my answering machine. I know someone tried to reach me. I just know it. It's even worse when the machine is on and I'm gone for six hours and there aren't any messages. I get this terrible feeling of rejection.
I used to hate answering machines—they intimidated me. Now I call my friends when I know they're not home, just so I can talk uninterrupted to their machines.

I hate it when I'm in a hurry and I call my friends to tell them one thing, real fast and they put their kid on the phone to tell me they went potty in the toilet. "Good shot. Now put your mother back on the phone!"

I hate when I call my gynecologist's office and his voice mail comes on and the greeting goes something like this: "That you for calling Specialists in OB/GYN. To process your call more efficiently, please press 1 if you think you're pregnant. If you think you're in labor, please press 2. If you think you have a yeast infection, just get some Monistat 7. We're too busy to help you."

I hate it when I put someone on hold and, when I return, they ask, "Who was that?" I think it's my business, that's who it was!

I hate it when I run to answer the phone, trip over the vacuum cleaner and, when I answer, it's a computer call.

I hate speakerphones. What a dirty trick!

I hate it when you can't hear someone's "Call Waiting" beep and they tell you they've got to go because they've got another call.

I never know if they're lying or if they just want to get rid of me.

I really hate it when someone puts me on hold and I get another call, which I can't take because I'm on hold.

I hate those really syrupy family greetings: "Hi, this is Judy, Jim, Jason and Jennifer. We can't come to the phone right now because we're too busy being a functional family. Please leave us a message and we'll get right back to you. Have a great day!" I can't resist. I must respond like this: "Hi, this is Phyllis from Travel World. Your family has been selected to receive a free trip to Disney World. Please call me back at 1-800-262-3333 and, BOOM, I hang up and just pray they don't have Caller ID.

Home Entertainment

Now there's another whole category of hating. I hate it when I'm wide-awake at night and there's nothing on television. I double-hate it when there are several good things on television and I can't keep my eyes open.

I hate it when I get all psyched up to watch a good movie on TV and realize I'm looking at last night's listings.

I hate it when I'm late recording something because I couldn't get the blank tape unwrapped in time. I also hate it when I can't find the time to watch something I taped because I didn't have time to watch it in the first place.

I hate it when I turn talk radio on to help me fall asleep and it's so interesting that it keeps me up half the night.

I hate it when I get emotionally involved with a song on the radio and it turns out to be a commercial.

I hate it when a great song comes on my car radio just as I'm pulling into my driveway.

I hate feeling like my mother when I watch MTV. I look at how these rock stars are dressed and I say, "I don't know. Is this the style now? Is that what the kids are wearing these days?"

I hate it when I pay to rent a movie and I don't watch it. I hate it even more when I don't return it on time and have to pay extra to not watch it.

Girl Stuff

My mother always said, "Powder and paint makes you what you ain't." You got that right, Mom. Being a woman is hard work. We have a whole job just making ourselves up. That's why I never understood men who like to cross-dress. Bless their hearts. Once you're in the rat race, you can't turn back. Because if you don't look good, you don't feel good. So, keep in mind, I love being a woman. But here are several things I hate about it. Also, for your reading pleasure, I've thrown in a few hates about dealing with the opposite sex and growing older.

I hate working out in a gym. It's hard enough getting dressed up for the day—who wants to put on make-up and get dressed, just to sweat? Who really wants to go to the gym anyway? I especially hate those young girls who work out for two hours and still look perfect. Personally, I do the Jewish girl's workout – buy designer clothes just because they're slenderizing.

I hate "chicks" who just had a baby and look like Twiggy. I hate it that I'm old enough to know who Twiggy is.

I hate it that I'm turning into my mother. While recently dining with my kids, the waitress asked me if I would like soup or salad and I replied, "Soup, with the dressing on the side." My kids cracked up and I now assume the role of the "idiot mother." I hate that.

I hate spending weeks searching for the perfect outfit to wear to a party and then, the night of the affair, I'm too lazy to get a pair of scissors to cut off the price tag. I just rip and pray.

I hate women who walk their dogs in the morning, wearing full make-up and a totally accessorized outfit. They look better at 7 a.m. than I do on a Saturday night.

I hate it when my husband doesn't believe me when I tell him I have nothing to wear. Just because I have a closet full of clothes doesn't mean I have something to wear. Right, girls?

Men never worry about what they're going to wear to a party (well, not straight men, anyway). I hate that—what to wear is a woman's biggest nightmare.

I hate that I have to take time out of my busy schedule to analyze invitations that come in the mail. It's ugly, it's beautiful,

Discover Me

it's cheap, it's expensive, too gaudy, too Jewish, too goyish; Oh, they're just having cocktails, no food? How tacky. Just appetizers, no dinner? What's the deal with that?

I hate it when I get done applying my mascara and sneeze—and it ends up all over my eyelids. I feel like Tammy Faye Baker.

I hate it when I'm going out and I have a long hair hanging from my chin, I can't find my tweezers and I just did my nails.

I hate it when I'm having one of my few good hair days – and it rains.

I hate getting a bad hair cut, color or perm. The last time I got my hair colored, it came out yellow and orange—it looked like a cheap rabbit coat. When this happens to me, I get a lump in my throat. I can't talk. I can't look in the mirror. It's hard enough for me to look in the mirror on a good day. Everyone in the salon is saying, "You look great, Phyllis." And I'm thinking, "This looks great? My husband's an optometrist. Maybe I should book you an appointment."

68

Worse than that is having to pay for it. "That will be $125."Plus, I have to leave a tip. I'm Jewish and, God forbid, I don't want anyone to think I'm cheap. Don't you think these gorgeous people in the salons would have enough sense to say, "Oh yeah. We really did screw you up bad. How much do you think that will cost you to get fixed in a good salon?"

Let's face it. I hate hair altogether. It either needs to be washed, cut, styled, permed, colored, conditioned or removed. Maybe Bruce Willis has the right idea. I hated my hair so much, I cut it off while writing this book. Actually, I had to whack it off with a weed eater. It was a fire hazard from all the perming and coloring.

I hate it when no one notices my expensive perfume, but as soon as I use cheap hair spray, everyone wants to know what fragrance I'm wearing.

I hate it when I buy a piece of clothing because it's on sale and it's a "great buy," and I end up never wearing it.

I hate it when "chicks" complain they can't wear a two-piece bathing suit anymore. I can't wear a one-piece anymore.

I hate being invited to a swimming party the day before my scheduled bikini wax. Actually, I don't know why I call it a bikini wax. I've never worn a bikini in my life. For me, it should be a one-piece skirt wax.

I hate when I walk into a party and I'm either under-dressed or over-dressed. All I want to say is "Excuse me. I'll be back in an hour."

I hate fluorescent lights. No matter how good you think you look, they totally blow your image.

I hate it when I forget to cut the "XL" tag off my new blouse and leave it hanging out for the whole world to see. Or when I've forgotten to take the price tag off a new blazer and it slips out of the collar at a cocktail party. Well, I'm sorry. It's hard for me to make up my mind on these big-ticket items.

I hate clothes marked "One Size Fits All."Oh, I don't think so!

Female impersonators—I hate 'em. The better they are, the more I hate 'em. They're gorgeous. I hate that I'll never look as good as a man in drag.

I hate it when I finally get a pair of blue jeans broken in after 4,000 washings and then they start to unravel.

I hate nouveau riche ladies who wave their hands in front of their faces to show off all their jewelry while they're talking to me. Some of these girls I know from high school and they're waving their hands under my nose, saying, "I can't believe that I ran into you. So what are you doing these days?" "What am I doing? I'm looking at your gaudy jewelry and your fake nails."

I hate that lying in the sun is bad for you. It used to be relaxing. Now it's a hot sweaty guilt trip.

I hate it when I think I look good and I don't run into anyone I know; I also hate it when I look like total crap—sweats, no make-up—and run into everyone I know. I also hate it when I run into someone and I've got on the same outfit I was wearing the last time I saw them.

I hate it when I buy something I think looks wonderful on me, get it home and it looks like I need to lose 20 pounds, which I do. I doubly hate it when I've worn a new outfit and my best friend says it makes me look heavier. Thanks, pal, I can't return it. Well...maybe I can.

I hate going shopping for clothes when I need new clothes so badly that I have nothing to wear shopping.

I hate it when I break a nail and my Super Glue is all dried up.

I hate people who look good in shorts and sandals the first hot day of the year. We're talking March here. "Oh, no, the sun's out. Time for a tan and a pedicure." I might be ready for this look by mid-June. Why didn't I start my "Thin Thighs in 30 Days program" 30 days ago?

I hate it when my $20 lipstick breaks the first time I use it.

I hate it when I just need one item at the make-up counter and the salesgirl tries to talk me into their "Free Gift" deal—you know, spend $98 on stuff you don't need to get a little bag of more stuff you don't need. I never end up using any of it.

I hate mail order catalogs. They have an 800 number to place your order and take your money—24 hours a day, seven days a week. But if you have a problem or need to return it, then you call 900-Good Luck!

I hate going to a party and someone is wearing the same outfit I have on. Then I found out she got hers on sale—and it's a smaller size!

I hate that I can't find time to take a time management course.

I hate it when I see my favorite pair of earrings in someone's nose.

I hate the fact that I'm forty-something. I finally got my skin cleared up and now I'm getting wrinkles. I'd like to thank my zits for making room for my crow's feet. I finally threw out all my Clearasil and now I'm stocking up heavily on RetinA. I used to drop acid. Now, I smear it on my face.

I hate it that my girlfriends' fathers don't look like fathers anymore. They look like grandfathers.

I hate it when I see a graying, balding, middle-aged guy with a pot belly who looks like should be at my father's poker game and then realize I graduated high school with him.

I hate having had two nervous breakdowns and I'm the most normal person in my family. My Aunt Selma had so many shock treatments, Union Electric used to bill her directly.

I hate going to the psychiatrist. It depresses me.

So, What's Next?

So, where am I now, you ask. It's a new century and I've collected some more stars on the resume on my path to having my star in the sidewalk in Hollywood.

I hosted a really popular segment on a local cable show called "What's Hot & New." My very handsome sidekick and I visited new hot spots, interviewed customers and owners, and made the places seem fun and interesting. My sidekick – I called him "my Ed McMahon" – was amazing, laughing at everything I said just when he should. Guess what? We were nominated for a local Emmy. I thought for sure we would be discovered! But we became just me when "Ed's" ego got too big and we split.

Not to worry. I still had my stand-up and, by some miracle, MGM/UA decides to shoot a Bill Murray movie in St. Louis. I auditioned for a part.

Okay, it wasn't "What About Bob" or "Groundhog Day." Mr. Murray had a run of a couple bad movies and "Larger Than Life" was one of them. His co-star was an elephant. They don't shoot many movies in St. Louis, so I knew this could be my big chance. Sure enough, I got a part. And one sunny day in May 1995, I found myself having make-up applied at 7 a.m. with Mr. Bill Murray just a couple of stools away. It was a perfect day.

I got to shoot a diner scene over and over and over, all day, with my hero. Bill and Phyl – I knew it was my lucky break. They actually used my scene for all the commercials and trailers, which was fun. I was going to be discovered in this part, five seconds as a waitress. I did get my private conversation with MBM (Mr. Bill Murray) and he was a complete inspiration. He was funny and off-the-wall all day long. I was kind of quiet and star-struck, afraid to say the wrong thing. But the film crew kept shooting me from the side and I thought you were supposed to see my face, head-on. So I asked the crew about it and MBM yells out, "Miss, Miss!" I could tell he was searching for a name, so I called back, "Miss Nobody." He was so funny, he yells out, "Miss Taylor wants to know about her close-up!"

The Hollywood premiere of "Larger Than Life" was Tuesday, Oct 29, 1996, in Los Angeles. I got my invitation the day before. I was frantic, trying to make a plane reservation and arrange for my cousin, who lives in L.A., to get me to this premiere. I just knew Penny Marshall or some other producer would be dying to meet me.

Well, it turns out Tuesday was the day of my son's Halloween play. He was going to be heartbroken if I didn't attend. Let's see – Hollywood premiere versus Halloween play. Well, you know how that story turned out. I saved $900 on the plane ticket and was a hit at Josh's second-grade Halloween play, signing autographs for his classmates.

My whole family went to the St. Louis premiere of "Larger Than Life" at the Esquire Theater the following night. We were waiting breathlessly for my scene. It went by in a flash, cut to next-to-nothing. Josh tapped me on the shoulder and gave me this all-knowing look. "Aren't you glad you didn't fly out to L.A. for that?"

That movie hit the Dollar rentals faster than my boobs hit my knees when I take my bra off. Bill went on to better things. I still get residual checks for a couple bucks every now and then, a decade later.

It's weird – even though I'm not famous, I have met three of my comedy idols. Besides Bill Murray and Rodney Dangerfield, I once ran into—well, made it a point to run into—Joan Rivers.

It was 1986 and she was playing Ceasars Palace. Someone at the hotel told me her limousine would be pulling in that Thursday at 2 p.m. My sister and I were out front at the appointed time and, sure enough, Joan Rivers arrived in a limo. We chatted, got her autograph and followed her through the hotel to her suite. I told her I was going to do stand-up and she wished me luck. My sister and I were dying to tell someone we had just met the great Joan Rivers, so we went to the pool bar outside. We laid the news on this couple who must have just come from the wedding chapel, they were totally all over each other. They didn't even hear what we were saying, just blew us off.

For the last 12 years, while I've been running around raising my family, doing stand-up, writing this book, writing a play, doing a little TV and making my five-second movie debut, I had a dream. I dreamed I would get discovered and make the whole country laugh. It was an escape from my everyday mother-wife existence.

Just recently, I made a huge discovery. I realized I was happy, whether I ever become famous or not. Thank God, I have raised happy kids, doggies and my happy, but now-disappointed husband. I should have kept my mouth closed and not promised him fame and fortune.

The good news is I discovered myself and God. I've discovered if you choose to have children, pets, spouses, it's going to take a lot of love, patience, hot water and soap. I've discovered that I'm not better than anyone else and it always pay to say please and thank-you with a smile. I've discovered the more you give, the more you receive. I've discovered how to be happy every day and that was the most wonderful discovery of all.

So again, I thank God for the opportunity to discover these things about myself and, if America still wants me, I'll be in the neighborhood.

Peace and Love,
Phyllis
www.PhyllisIsFunny.com
phyllisisfunny@aol.com

Printed in the United States
70807LV00002B/1-249

9 781595 940667